Lady Georgiana Chatterton

Lady May

A Pastoral

Lady Georgiana Chatterton

Lady May
A Pastoral

ISBN/EAN: 9783337108489

Printed in Europe, USA, Canada, Australia, Japan

Cover: Foto ©ninafisch / pixelio.de

More available books at **www.hansebooks.com**

LADY MAY.

[The Copyright is reserved.]

LADY MAY.

A PASTORAL.

BY

GEORGIANA LADY CHATTERTON.

LONDON:
THOMAS RICHARDSON AND SON;
DUBLIN, AND DERBY.
MDCCCLXIX.

LADY MAY.

PART I.

A HOMELY valley in a Midland shire
   Before my grateful memory doth rise—
A scene most English in our Land of Homes,
Far hid from din of factory or mart;
A village where the church's Norman tower
Still speaks of steadfast faith to later times,
And seems with bold and massive strength to guard
The greater glories of a later art
Which pierced those mullioned windows down the nave
In good King Edward's reign. 'Twas in this vale
Some forty years ago, a couple dwelt,
An aged loving pair and prosperous—
Yet not indeed with this their lot content;
For childless they had been, and Nelly Rolfe,
The dame of whom I write, was young at heart,
Altho' full three score summers she had seen,

As when she married Jonas in her prime:
And sunny was her face, as if all life
Had been a summer's day. She ne'er looked sad
Except when Jonas tarried at the inn
Full late, to hear, he said, the latest news—
For then 'twas near the end of wars with France,
When for the groaning lands was freedom won.

  A stone's throw from the church was Jonas' house,
Its gable to the little street was turned:
In front a garden lay; its well-kept beds
Were gay with crimson tulip and jonquil,
And many a gaudy flower or sweetest herb
Our forebears loved, but now too seldom seen.
The beehives, sheltered by the clipped yew hedge,
Looked towards the sun, and at the farther end
An arbour decked with shells was seen,—'twas there
The Dame full oft with village gossips talked.
Well loved was she, and sought from far and near
By all who wanted sympathy or help:
For she in youth had lived as nursery-maid
At Morland Hall, and there had learned some skill
In leechcraft as 'twas practised in those days.

  There too, it was that she had learned to love,

E'en more than youth is wont, all helpless babes,
Their winning ways and wiles, the first faint cry
Of babyhood: its sudden bitter griefs
And joys so innocent. And even when
Young Jonas, who had loved her ten long years,
Would wait no longer and her promise claimed—
She sighed to leave them, though her heart was his.

   The great folks grieved to lose her from the hall,
And all the children wept till they were told
That they should often see their own loved Nell
In her new pretty cottage, just beyond
The South Park Gates.

                    One of the olden type
Was Jonas' house; built, like the Manor House,
Of grey hewn stone—the little sheltering porch
Surmounted with a date that told the year
Just after England's Charles had lost his head.
'Twas said the stones, like those of Morland Hall,
Came from the ruined abbey, in the midst
Of that fair vale, and erst were brought with care
And loving labour, in remoter times
When England's faith was one, by hooded monks
From sea-washed cliffs on Purbeck's distant shore.

One evening, in the merry month of May,
Old Nelly in her arbour sat alone.
The news had come of some great battle gained,
And much she feared that Jonas, in his glee,
Would tarry long, and by his friends beguiled,
Would e'en forget himself, as he had done,
Alas! too oft of late, and deeply drink,
Well knowing that they had no child, no heir
For whom to save—none who might good or ill
From good or bad example pattern take.

And, in her bitter disappointment, she
Began to think that all would have been right
If they had had a child to love and teach:
Then sighed, and as the sun went down she knelt
And wept hot tears of bitter self-reproach,
Praying that God would her complaints forgive.
She conned her sacred hymns, and, musing read
The chapters in St. John she loved the best,
Then laid her down to sleep, for well she knew
That Jonas, finding her awake, would chafe,
Deeming himself the cause of her unrest—
Then say 'twas hard. Full peacefully she slept
And dreamed a dream. She thought a child was born,

LADY MAY.

A lovely smiling babe; nor marvelled she,
For nought seems strange in dreams, at what was not
In nature nor in possibility.
She seemed as young as on her wedding day—
Her three score years, her faded wrinkled face,
Her Jonas's feebler steps, she reck't them not—
But holy joy and thankfulness to God
Were all she felt. For there the little one
Lay smiling in her arms—a maiden babe
With eyes of deep dark blue, like the loved child
(Young Geraldine Adare) whom she had nursed
In early youth at the old Manor House.
And now she felt the new-born baby's breath,
Its sweet warm breath upon her cheek, the clasp
Of little clinging fingers round her own—
Then woke. So vivid was the dream, that still
There seemed the gentle pressure on her breast,
And still her fingers tingled with the touch
Of baby hands. So blissful was the feel
She longed to sleep again, and closed her eyes,
Then opened them, and almost hoped to find
A living infant in her loving arms.

The room with Eastern sunbeams now was bright,

And so she knew it was full time to rise
And make her husband's breakfast. Hastily
She dressed, and then went down, but was so wrapt
In memory of her dream, that in her work
She made unwonted blunders—burnt the toast
And spoiled the oaten cakes.

"What ails thee, Nell?"
Her husband asked; and then she smiling, mused,
But nought would say; for in her youthful days
She heard that dreams, if in the morning told,
Will ne'er come true. And then she laughed outright;
"Ah, how could such a dream come true for me!
For *me*," she thought, "now in my sixtieth year?"

"What ails thee, wench?" said Jonas. "Art thou dazed?
Hast seen a ghost? See, thou hast burnt the cakes,
And overturned the milk, and spoiled the toast!"

"I've only overslept myself," she said;
"Mayhap the flour is bad: I'll to the mill
And get some new. Besides, hast thou not heard,
'More haste, worse speed.' So often used to say
My Lady at the Manor House. Ah, me,
I wish I knew what came to that poor child,

My darling Ina—if so be she lives.
Now, haste thee, Jonas—hark, the hour hath chimed."
The dame would have him gone—for once she wished
To be alone, for once—that she might muse
And think and muse again upon her dream,
And seek the place where she had seemed to be.

  She knew the spot full well—'twas near her home,
Her own old home beyond the Abbey Ponds
Near Dowling's Mill. Her father there had lived:
Dearly she loved the spot, and oft had thought
In all the world there could be nought so fair
As Morland Abbey, and its great oak woods.
And so, her husband gone at last, she donned
Her cloak and hood, then hastened to the vale.

PART II.

THE sun was shining on the highest tower
   While yet the ruined cloisters were in shade;
So Nelly knew 'twas early morning still,
Although impatience made her think it late.
For like a sundial to her practised eye
Were all the beauteous features of the vale;
The rippling stream, the dark o'erhanging woods,
The dome-like downs, furze-gilded, rising fair.
   And, as a child, she knew when it was time
In summer morns for school, because the knight
In armour lying, on the altar tomb,
Then seemed to smile with joy, as if he felt
The morning sun that slanted o'er his face,
And warmed, as Nelly thought, his hands upraised
In ceaseless prayer. At noon he was in shade,
And then she thought he frowned; for stern and sad
The marble features grew. And when the mists
Of twilight fell, she was almost afraid

LADY MAY.

Of coming nigh: she fancied that his hands
Moved slowly, and that murmured sentences
And whispers strange passed through his marble lips.

   Yet even then, at all times, light or dark,
She loved the spot, and often did she come
To think of those whom living she had loved,
And grieved for still.

                  It was a lovely scene:
Most English in the ruined Abbey lone
That stamped a page in history's awful book
With mutilated Beauty and marred Faith;
Fair witness to foul deeds of enmity
(By abstract Faith since made respectable)
Which armed a Tyrant's will. Most English! aye,
For seldom do we see in other lands
A sacred building, reared at such a cost
Of wondrous art, for centuries remain
Untouched—but perishing in calm decay.

   And now the May morn sun was shining bright,
As Nell had seen it clearly in her dream.
The miller's gabled house was yet in shade,
But the mill stream that through the valley wound
Ran glistening in its rays. The gnarlèd oaks

With yellow budding leaves, above her head
Were tipped with golden light, as in her dream
They had appeared above the new-born child.

With wondering awe she hastened on, and passed
The miller's house, nor thought to get her meal;
But clambered up a winding path that led
Along the steep o'erhanging primrose banks,
Beside the little rivulet, that seemed
To dance and smile in gladness, rushing down.
Still further up she went, with quickened steps;
For more and more the windings of the vale,
The budding flowers, the sunshine and the trees,
All that she saw, looked like her happy dream.
Nor did she stop till to the spot she came;
There narrowest the gorge—there shadows dark
Of branches interlaced, lay on the deep
And quiet waters of the High Oak Pond.

The place she knew right well; for years ago
When yet a child, she once had ventured in
To pluck the water lilies shining there
Like cups of gold beneath the mid-day sun,
Then slipped and lost her footing: for the pond
Was treacherous and deep.   But Jonas heard

Her cry of agony, and flew to help.
" Perchance that's why I always loved the place,"
Thought she. " And then to feel I was so near
To death that day! But brave and bold he was
My Jonas, aye and is, and he could swim;
Dear! how his eyes did shine, I mind right well,
Like stars, the moment that he caught me up
And bore me to the bank."

                                                        She sat her down
To rest awhile upon the mossy turf,
And then the memories of by-gone days
Came crowding through her mind so rapidly,
And with such marked distinctness, that in truth
She, for the time, well nigh forgot her dream.
She thought again of all her gay young days,
When she was living at the Manor House;
How deeply she had loved the children there,
And most of all the little Geraldine.
She was the youngest of those bright Adares,
And loveliest. From birth Nell tended her,
And saw with a triumphant pride and joy
Her darling reach her lovely sixteenth year.
But that was thirty years before. And then

They left the place, and never since that day
Had Nelly seen, or scarcely heard of her.
Now some were dead she knew, and some were worse,
And rumours vague in after years had come
That Geraldine had sailed to India's clime
With a young soldier who had won her heart.

Ah! little truly had she heard of them
Since that dark day when they were chased from home,
Compelled for heavy debts to fly in shame,
And hide their poverty in foreign lands;
For the Adares had lived beyond their means.
This Nelly knew, and she had dreaded long
Some fatal ending to their revels gay,
And heedless, though perhaps good natured, wish
To see all others glad. But it had proved
Far worse than this; for when the old squire died,
He left, besides a heritage of debts
Which e'en that large estate could never pay,
A sullied name, disgraceful to Adares.

Ancestral relics then were seized by Jews,
The Hall dismantled, and the pictures sold,
And priceless hordes of by-gone centuries
Were scattered. This was all the neighbours knew.

The place had been shut up for many years :
The terrace steps were overgrown with moss,
The garden had become a wilderness,
And rats, the only inmates of the house,
Holding dim revels on the inlaid floors,
Scared passers-by with noises weird and strange :
While bats behind the wainscot squeaked and chirped,
And flitted round the carven ceilings rare,
Or flapped with dusky wings the moonlit pane.
A scene of desolation : sad but meet ;
Harmonious with the fate of the Adares.

Old Nelly could not bear to see it now ;
Yet day by day failed not to think on those
Whom she had loved so well ! 'Twas passing strange
That nought was heard of them. She could believe
At times in the mysterious malison
Which she had heard had been pronounced on those
Whose ancestors had seized the abbey lands,
And ruthless helped to desecrate the tombs
Of holy men who had been buried there.

But Jonas aye had scouted that belief,
And said those Popish priests had met their due,
Nor could he think it had been wrong to take

The consecrated stones for Morland Hall,
As some maintained, and urged that the Adares
Had never prospered since ; nor e'er had passed
A generation without fearful ills
Descending on that mansion and its lords.

"And we are childless too," would Nelly say,
"I wonder if it be because our house
Was built o' th' Abbey stones ?   Alack-a-day !
I would it had not been ; and Jonas too,
He got it from an uncle : ne'er a child
The old man had, though he was wedded twice."

Thus buried in the past old Nelly mused,
And scarce the present scene her eye discerned,
Nor saw the water lilies' golden leaves,
Nor their reflection in the dimpled pond
On which her eyes were fixed.
                                                    But suddenly
A far-off sound she heard, which made her start,
And quickly look around, for oh ! 'twas like
The baby cry that she had, dreaming, heard.
Yes ! 'twas the same.   She upward strained her eyes
To gaze where slanting sunbeams bathed in light
The steep high bank, as if she could believe

A babe were truly there, amid the wild
And tangled branches of the bramble rose.

   The bank had been a quarry once; but now
'Twas overgrown with bushes, which had clung
And spread their roots amid the clefts of rock.
There, often, in her childhood she had climbed.

   Again that plaintive sound was heard, and then
She hastened on, regardless of her years—
Of bramble sharp or backward sliding stone:
As rapidly she climbed, as when in youth
Her eager hands had gathered blue bells there.

   Nor halted she for breath, nor felt fatigue
Once in that long ascent. It seemed as though
A youthful vigour for the while returned
Through eagerness to reach the spot, and search
The topmost rosebush, which, as she approached,
Looked e'en as it had looked in her strange dream.

   With trembling hands she moved the slender boughs,
And lo! 'twas lying there, the lovely babe
Whom, dreaming, she had seen the night before,
Its tiny dimpled arms to her outstretched.
No broidered baby robes its form bedecked,
A woollen cloth the only garb it wore,

And in a basket of rude work it lay,
For bed—or coffin, as most probably
It might have chanced. No mark of any kind,
To shew its parentage or name she found,
Or help conjecture to a clue.

      Most strange!
The slender branches had sustained its weight,
Its little darling weight—more precious far,
More precious to old Nelly's yearning heart
Than all the gold this weary world contained.
There it had lain suspended, 'mid the boughs,
The swaying branches of the bramble rose:
Just o'er the deepest part of High Oak Pond:
A breath had blown it down!

      She, shuddering gazed
On the stone wall that bounded, far above
The old high road from Normantower. 'Twas built,
She well remembered, many years before,
Because 'twas there, where steepest the descent
That one dark night the coach was overturned,
And fell straight down into the High Oak Pond.
And some were drowned, and some were saved, of those
Who travelled in the old stage coach that night.

She thought, and at the notion held her breath,
And pressed the babe still closer in her arms,
That some one from the road had thrown it o'er
The parapet: intending that the child
Should fall into the stagnant silent pond;
And thus its very birth might be concealed.

And then she softly kissed its little cheek,
But scarce allowed herself another look
While standing o'er that perilous abyss,
Lest through the trembling of her joyous heart,
Or accidental footslip, she should chance
To let the infant fall. Much longer time
Was passed in the descent. Slowly she came
With cautious steps, and arm extended out,
To keep the prickly brambles from the Babe,
Who had, unconscious of its peril great,
Begun to crow with that soft cooing sound,
So like the babies at the Manor House.

At last she reached the level ground, below
The primrose bank that bordered High Oak Pond:
There sitting down she well nigh swooned away
For joy, and present sense of peril past;
Then found in tears of happiness relief,

And tried to give God thanks, (though scarce could she
In her great weakness frame befitting words,)
That this her life-long wish He had fulfilled.
  But presently she trembled—vaguely feared
That all might prove a dream. She longed to show
The babe to Jonas; yet was loth to move,
Dreading the spell (for so it seemed) might fade,
As when at early morn she had awoke
From her mysterious dream. And then she laughed
At such vain fears, rose suddenly, and went
With tremulous quick steps adown the vale,
Passed by the river, and the miller's house,
Thence to the village. But she still concealed
Beneath the ample folds of cloak and hood
Her precious burden from the greeting friends
And neighbours whom she met, nor said a word
E'en to her brother Bevis, who passed by.
  "Good Nell," said he, "here let me take thy meal;
'Tis heavy, dame, and thou art tired and hot:
I saw thee turn to Dowling Mill."

                                          "Not so,
Not so," she said; "let be: I'm just at home."
Then hurried on. And half aloud he said,

"Whatever ails her now? She looks as though
She'd seen a ghost or found a crock of gold."

   Safely arrived at home, she dressed the child
In little clothes that once were Geraldine's,
And had been treasured up for many years
In rose-leaf scented cabinet, her gift.
And then she sat her down and rocked the babe
Till Jonas should return at noon to dine;
The while she laughed, or mused with joyous heart,
And pictured to herself his great surprise.

PART III.

FOUR years have passed since Nelly's happy dream,
   And now the little May, (for by that name
The babe discovered on that bright May morn
Was christened), had begun to grow apace.
Old Jonas had indeed been overjoyed
To see that lovely babe on his return,
Yet thought it right to make its finding known
In all the country round, lest, as he said,
Its parents might be grieving for its loss.
   And Nell had often trembled, nay, e'en yet
She trembled at the thought. "Ah, well-a-day!"
She said, and pressed it closer still, and kissed
Its little blooming cheek, and sighed to think
How much she wished that search might fruitless prove.
For sure 'twas wrong, as Jonas said, to dread
That the loved child should her lost parents find.
   "Of gentle birth, she is, I wot," said Nell,
"She is so like the children at the hall.

See, how she arches oft her snowy neck,
And moves her tiny hand in proud command;
Besides, her winning ways and stately air
Might well become the daughter of a prince."
The village children called her Lady May,
Half in derision, half in awe, and yet
Obeyed her slightest wish, and strove to please
The winsome wayward child whom all did love.

Thus time passed with her uneventfully
Until her fifteenth year, when Jonas died.
Then Nelly feared that May might soon be left
All unprotected in this troublous world,
So full of varied peril, seeing that
Herself might follow soon. And who should then,
Ah! who indeed, protect that orphan child!

Her nephew, Reuben Bevis, by the mill,
Her brother's only son, had lost his wife;
She, dying, left a child whom May loved well,
And tended, teaching all the lore she knew.
And Reuben, grateful for such kindly help,
Entranced, moreover, by her beauty rare,
Began to love, yet scarce acknowledged it,
So far above him seemed the stately May.

He felt he ne'er could win her. No, not he;
As possible 'twould be to grasp the moon,
As possible to seize the morning star,
In golden glory pulsing through the vast
Dim arc of heaven, and joyful hastening on
To meet her lord the sun. So Reuben felt.

About that time repeated rumours came
That soon the Manor House would be restored.
The Viscount Hollingbourne possessed it now;
He, next of kin to Reginald Adare,
(The Squire's youngest born in battle slain),
Was heir-at-law—for all were dead and gone
Whom Nelly knew. His was the eldest branch
And richest of that old and honoured race,
Styled Barons of Adare and Norman Tower,
From feudal times. His grandsire had been made
A Viscount for the passing of some Bill
That kept a tottering Ministry in place
One session more.
     Some twenty miles away
Was Norman Tower, the Viscount's stately home,
And Nelly knew that they had been of old
Unfriendly to the Squires of Morland Vale.

But when the neighbours said that he would come,
That Morland Manor House would smile once more,
And merry jest and voice of man and maid
Be heard in its dim chambers, and sweet songs
Resound in the long silent banquet hall;
While cheerful steps would cross its dainty floors,
Waking fair echoes of the olden time;
Old Nell rejoiced, anon she somewhat feared,
'Twere not, perchance, so well for May.

"As yet,
No gentlefolks," thought she, " have known my child;
And strangers, seeing her, must marvel much
That village maiden should such beauty boast.
Then foolish vanity at praise unsought
Might steal its baneful poison through her heart."
Lord Hollingbourne she knew had lost his wife:
Some said he killed her by his passions wild;
Yet that he loved his only daughter Blanche
Now in her nineteenth year. Two sons he had,
The eldest born was wild and like his sire,
But Claude, the second son, fair promise gave,
And seemed a noble nature to possess.
All this she heard, and more, that made her dread

The Viscount and his heir, and almost wish
That Morland Manor House should aye remain
In desolation.
   But, at length a day
Was fixed upon when Blanche alone would come
To take possession of her future home.
The Viscount was in France. But yet the dame
Willed not that May should join her village friends,
Who donned their best attire, and hastened up
Beyond the old Park gates, to see her come,
The fair young Madam in her coach-and-four,
Rejoicing that the long deserted Hall
Would be alive again. May long had loved
Its gables peaked, and ivy-covered walls,
And oft had lingered in its grass-grown courts,
And peeped into the rooms, or climbed aloft
The quaint old buttresses of stone, and gazed
Through answering windows, on the centre court.
In stately rooms like these she longed to dwell,
With ceilings high and beautifully carved,
With mullioned windows lit by storied glass,
And polished floors with diverse woods inlaid.
 Oft she had traced with ready pen the form

Of pendant boss and complicated curve,
Of figures quaint around the chimneypiece
In old black oak. She drew them one by one
From recollection when she sat at home,
While Nell looked on amazed, to see portrayed
The room where last she saw young Geraldine.

The maiden longed to see, and welcome too,
The future inmates of the place she loved;
And wondered why, on that eventful day,
Old Nelly held her back and looked so grave,
While all the rest were glad—while the old bells
Rang out a merry peal, that almost seemed
To shake the grey church tower. Yes, it was strange.
While Susan Dean and farmer Dowling's girl,
And many more, had donned their Sunday dress,
And flocked along the old high road that led
To the South Lodges, bearing garlands gay,
To greet the future Lady of the Hall.

But Nelly Rolfe and May remained at home
In their lone cottage garden all that eve;
Upon an oaken bench they sat at work,
Within the porch close by the village street,
For warm the even was—May longed for air—

And pale the maiden looked to Nell's fond eyes.
Anon the colour mounted to her cheeks,
As starting up she looked with anxious gaze
Adown the village street. "What ails thee, child?"
The dame enquired, but soon the reason saw.
A cloud of dust—then outriders appeared—
And then an open carriage quickly passed
Quite close to where they stood. And May could see
A fair young face and beauteous eyes that looked
Into her own with pleased and glad surprise.
'Twas but a moment, yet old Nelly Rolfe
Saw that the lady had remarked her child,
And felt that e'en for good or evil, Blanche
Would henceforth hold an influence over May.

All the next night she scarce could sleep for care,
So vivid were the changes possible
In May's young life, and yet amid her fears
She hoped that Blanche Adare would prove a friend,
A real friend as long as both should live.
But, ah! the father and the wild young heir,
Her heart within her sank at thought of them;
But earnestly she prayed and cast her care
On Him who had bestowed that child on her.

And May was wakeful too—and, wondering, thought
Of all that Mistress Blanche would do—what room
She had selected for her own, and where
She meant to pass the sunny morning hours;
If in the southern oriel, looking down
Upon the terraced garden—there perchance
She might be walking on the morrow's eve,
And May might see her. Musing thus, the child
Dropt off asleep, and in her blissful dreams
The stranger lady's eyes looked kinder still
Than to her waking gaze they had appeared.

'Twas late when they awoke. The dame rose first,
And hastened to her darling's bed, to see
If she were safe, half smiling at her fears—
Yet vaguely anxious—more and more convinced
That in the onward course of time, the race,
The stranger race of these unknown Adares,
For good or ill would influence her child.

It chanced that on this very afternoon,
While May was busied with some household work,
Which then, as ever, she obedient wrought
With playful and glad willingness for Nell,
And with such graceful skill that nought appeared

Unseemly, mean, or vulgar, that she touched,
The strange presentiment appeared like truth.

While May was rubbing bright the parlour floor,
Whose old oak boards she loved to polish well,
Speeding along a leaden-weighted brush
With dancing step while humming some wild air,
Her cotton gown, its sleeves and skirt tucked up,
Appearing as if made express to show
The pretty rounded arm and fairy foot,
She saw reflected in the polished boards
A figure past the open casement glide,
Then blushing, turned to look, convinced that step
So hushed and graceful was no village girl's.
'Twas Blanche Adare. And she had come to see
The wondrous pretty maiden, whose fair face
Had left its impress on her memory,
So that she straight had asked, " What people lived
In the stone cottage by the village green ?"
And they had told her 'twas the widow Rolfe,
With her adopted daughter, Lady May.
They said, moreover, that the Dame had lived
As nurse in days of yore at Morland Hall,

LADY MAY.

And then in her old age had found this child
According to a dream.
      Blanche heard much more,
And what she heard confirmed the sudden thought,
That it were best that May should ne'er suspect
She might not have been born a peasant's child,
And therefore, ent'ring now, Blanche turned and spoke
To Nelly most, and many questions asked,
Touching the old Adares, as if she liked
To hear their praises told—which pleased the Dame.
But oft she looked at May, and said, at length,
" You'll bring her to the hall, then you can see
All we are doing to the place you love ;
The pictures, too, from foreign lands renowned,
Although you may not like them, Dame, so well
As the old portraits long ago dispersed."
 Then Nelly answered with a curtsey low,
That she would bring her child to Morland Hall ;
But added somewhat that disclosed her fears,
Lest discontented with her humble home
The child should grow. Blanche understood her fears
And motioning to May to cull some flowers
(As yet were none at Morland Hall), she watched

The maiden tripping down the gravel path
Till out of hearing. Then she whispered low
In Nelly's ear. "Fear not : I guess it all.
Depend on me, no hint shall she receive
Of the suspicion which we all must feel,
That she is other than appears—not one ;
Nor learn to love the mother less, whose care
And guardianship has made her what she is,
Most lovely in her mind, and form, and face,
And pure as driven snow. You trust me, dame ?"
Nell curtseyed low, and strove to feel content
That May should often visit Morland Hall ;
And as the days rolled on, she learned herself
To love fair Blanche, and wholly trust in her ;
But vainly sought a likeness in her face
To the lost owners—dear with all their faults—
Of Morland Manor and its fair broad lands.
More like by far to the beloved old race
Was little May. She had the same blue eyes,
Dark fringed with raven lashes, and the skin
So pearly fair ; the eyebrows long and fine,
Like those that arched o'er Geraldine's sweet eyes ;

The swan-like throat, the graceful springing step,
Her voice, her laughter e'en, resembled theirs.

And she had grown more like, as years rolled on,
Till Nelly often started when she looked
Upon her suddenly; and wondering mused
If possibly she were indeed the child
Or grandchild of lost Geraldine; then sighed
And sadly smiled at such surmise.

        And May
Loved well the grave tall Blanche, and strove each day
To please and cheer her; often marvelling why
She should be sad in such a princely home,
Surrounded by all beauteous things, with means
And will to make so many glad.

         'Twas true
She was alone: her brother came not there;
Her father still remained in foreign lands;
And yet his absence did not seem to cause
This sorrow. May was wise in gracious tact;
Her mind was now expanding day by day
To stronger entity, and she had seen
That Blanche, at mention of her father's name,
Would start and grow more pale, although she spoke

With reverence and filial love of him,
And now and then would say quite suddenly,
"Oh think of him in all thy prayers to heaven,
For if thou lovest me thou must love him."
And then a tear would tremble in her eye,
And she would sigh and muse abstractedly,
Seeming much older than her nineteen years,
As one who overmuch had thought and felt.
Yet she was beautiful; although at times
A shade of sternnesss clouded her high brow—
A shadow soon dispelled, and rarest seen
When May was near. "Dear little Lady May,"
She oft would call her, yet she kept her word,
Nor ever hinted what so many thought,
That May was other than appeared.

        Meanwhile
Young Reuben Bevis watched with anxious eyes
To see how May would bear this change of scene:
And whether she would still appear to care,
As once, for his poor child, and wish to nurse
And teach her as of yore. Or if, perchance
Her grand new friend, and all the retinue
Of gorgeous servants now at Morland Hall,

Would make her proud, and she would cease to care
For aught so dull and humble as his home.
 And yet he never spoke his fears, nor seemed
Such change to dread ; but Nelly read his thoughts,
And counselled him that he should not despair.
Truly o'er-anxious was the dame that May
Should be betrothed ere long—nay, even spoke
Thereon to Blanche, one day at Morland Hall,
When quite alone with her, by accident
Of time and circumstance, long since forgot.
Blanche looked up quickly, and replied in haste,
As if relieved from some great care or dread :
" He has a noble heart, I think ; I'm sure
He cares for her : I have remarked him oft,
When she has passed his cottage door with me."
These words old Nelly heard with thankful joy :
They reassured, and helped her to decide ;
For she had partly feared that Blanche would think
Her nephew was not good enough for May,
As, sooth to say, she often thought herself,
Though now that she was growing very old
She longed to see her safely wed with one
Who would at least protect and love her well.

All this old Nelly pondered, and she knew
That May well loved her nephew's little child,
And told herself that it were surely best
For May to wed young Reuben, nor to wait.
She reasoned e'en as worldly mothers do,
Unconscious that she might be doing wrong;
And guided by the self-same instinct—such
As makes the so-called worldling plot and plan
In ball-room, opera, or country house,
With baneful bonhomie, both try to do
The thing they deem most likely to ensure
Their child's prosperity. Then is it fair
To breathe forth indiscriminate contempt
And loud denunciations 'gainst one class
Upon that score, as commonly is done
In books and table-talk? But let that pass.

  One morning Blanche, by Nelly's earnest wish,
(Half stammered and half hinted nervously,)
Outspoke the case to May in sudden words,
As if she forced herself to utter them.
May heard her gravely—then felt almost stunned,
And bursting into tears she hid her face,
Yet marvelled why she wept, for she believed

That Reuben was the best, the very best,
Of all mankind. "Yes, I am sure he is,"
She said at length to Blanche amid her tears,
Unconscious that she had not spoken yet.
"He is so good, I ought to be right glad
To think that I could give him happiness."
And then she trembled and grew pale, and looked
Upon the view she knew and loved so well,
From Blanche's oriel window, down the vale.
Intently on the well-known scene she gazed,
As if its loveliness could e'en restore
The gladness she had lost. But all in vain:
The landscape was the same—the joy was gone.
Then turning to the pictures that she loved,
She sought if any happiness were left;
But these too failed—they gave not back her joy.
"Perchance," thought she, "I see not for my tears."
Again she wondered why she should have wept,
Remembering that to grieve was not her wont,
That she had never wept indeed before,
Except when Jonas died.
     It seemed that Blanche
Divined her feelings partly, partly hoped

'Twas only the first thought and the surprise.
Yet wished indeed, if otherwise, that May
Almost in spite of such, might acquiesce;
And firmly soothed and led the grieving girl
With hints more felt than heard; the blissful lot
Of one—like May, for instance—loved through life
Within that happy valley, freed from care,
Loved by a true heart, faithfully and well.
" And when my father comes," said Blanche, " perhaps
He will not stay here long, and then I fear
It will be lonely for you when I'm gone.
And Nelly too is old, aye very old,
And in the course of nature cannot live
Much longer in this world of death and grief,
For such it is, dear May: a weary world
Though happy you have been, and never yet
Have learned to feel its sadness."

                              But May sighed
And thought 'twas sad indeed, a weary world;
Yet wondered that she had not thought it so
Until that hour. But then quite suddenly
A retrospective insight, full and swift,
Of her own life, so far as it had reached,

Revealed before her consciousness that she
Had sometimes felt aweary, sometimes grieved
And longed for somewhat vaguely. Could it be
That those dim longings and regrets foreshowed
Life's incompleteness—the attainable?
And then she thought (though not in form of words)
That it was very sad, this old, old world
So new to her self-consciousness, and tried
For resignation to breathe forth a prayer,
But scarcely could be said to pray, and then
Resolved to make the best of it, that course
Which lies between rebellion and despair,
From resignation just as far removed
As from resistance. And again she wished
Most passionately to acquire the hope
Of happiness above, for now it seemed
That even heavenly life had waxen dim
And doubtful to her faith.

* * * * * *

Nell had her wish.
May tacitly consented: either then
Or at some later hour indefinite,

But on the self-same day. The possible
Resolved into the probable, and thence
Into the vaguely certain, thence full soon
Into the certain; coloured by the light
Of pleasant intercourse, and softly toned
By Reuben's absence (he was absent then
For some few days) and by his earnest love,
Which absence made congenial. 'Twas arranged
Not by persuasion, properly so-called,
But rather through disposal of her mind
By Blanche's, and of Blanche's by the shape
Of circumstance, and what she called Nell's wish.

 Thus was arranged the compact which must bind
These two for lifetime: all was settled, e'en
To Reuben's wedding day. The tenth of June
Was named, agreed to, fixed in such brief time
As would have been unseemly; were it not
That Nelly so desired.

      Then Blanche Adare
Both chose and gave the wedding dress, and said
That she would have a village fete that day,
And all the girls and boys, May's youthful friends,
Should gifts, by her selected, have from Blanche,

Who would, moreover, give gay new attire
To all who were invited to the feast.

  And so the time most rapidly sped on,
In preparations made and lengthened out
By Blanche; and when the first of June had dawned
In sunlight warmly tinged with summer hues,
May passively looked forth, and sighed and thought
" The tenth too soon will come."

                              That selfsame eve
She sat in Blanche's room at sunset hour,
That room from whence the eye could reach far down
The valley to the ruined abbey towers;
And sought with her untutored skill to draw
The much-loved scene. Partly that she might have
Its image near her in her future home—
In part that she might occupy her mind
Without reflection. There was on the right
An avenue that led to Morland Hall;
And as she looked, endeavouring to portray
Its silver beech-stems tinted with the sun,
A carriage at the farther end appeared,
All white with dust.

                " Who comes so late!" said Blanche,

"My father would have written, if this night
He purposed coming." Then she trembled much,
Turned pale, and said, "Stay here till I return."

She left the room: May knew she passed adown
The winding staircase in that southern wing,
Which opened on the groined Banquet Hall,
And saw her on the terrace soon emerge,
Then pass along it to the carven gates.

Meanwhile the carriage stopped, and from it sprang
A graceful, handsome youth, resembling Blanche,
Who clasped her lovingly with eager arms.

"It is her brother," May surmised, and watched,
As on the fragrant terrace arm-in-arm
She saw them slowly pace. And presently
Blanche pointed to the oriel of her room,
And raised her eyes to May, who sudden felt
That they were speaking of her, and she blushed.

And Claude looked quickly up—his eyes met May's—
He looked as Blanche had looked that gladsome eve
When in the village street, a year before,
They first had met; but his blue eyes expressed
More happiness, or rather they betrayed
No sign of sorrow. May drew back, and blushed

More consciously; meanwhile a sense of joy,
Vague, undefined, was growing in her heart.

  Some minutes passed—then voices met her ear,
And happy footsteps coming up the stairs—
The door flew open, and he came with Blanche
Into the oriel chamber, as the sun
Was sinking down behind the quarry hill,
'Mid gold and purple vapours. Only once
He looked at May, then, turning, praised her sketch,
And praised the wedding dress which Blanche brought
     forth,
With strange persistance, to display it all—
The golden brooch—the bows—which she had placed
Upon its stomacher, with her own hand.
He smiled and said that Blanche had done it well,
But scarcely looked at it. "'Tis growing late,
And I must send you home, dear child," said Blanche.
Claude started then, as if his thoughts had been
Strangely absorbed—again he looked at May—
A gaze with more of sadness than of joy—
As if he strove to read her inmost mind,
Or print her every feature on his own.
"Farewell," he said, "and may your lot be blessed."

He took her hand, and then, with such an air
Of high respect, he raised it to his lips,
That May was all amazement—almost thought
It was a happy dream, nor would she move
Or even speak, lest the unwonted charm
Should melt away. A moment—he was gone—
And she was left filled with a sudden fear,
That in this world she ne'er should see him more.

But Blanche embraced her tenderly, and said,
In tones that sounded like her brother Claude's,
" Now come, dear child, for I must take you home;
Rejoiced am I that you have seen him once—
My brother—for, alas! he leaves me soon
To visit the far south. He came to-day
To bid farewell, and see the Manor House."

Blanche took her home—walked even to the door
Of Nelly's house—conversing all the while
With rapid utterance of many things,
But saying nought of Claude, whose image grew
In May's young heart, unconsciously the while.
That night she could not sleep for very joy,
Or rather joyousness of fancy—such
As is not recognized though felt. It seemed

That years had passed in that long happy eve,
And that the sun were shining bright and clear
All through that starless night. She feared to sleep,
Lest in her sleep she should forget her bliss,
Then wake to find it but a dream. At length,
When day began to dawn she sank to sleep—
To sleep but not to rest. The scene was changed;
Dark figures round her moved, while in their midst
Stood Reuben pale and haggard; and he gazed
With miserable eyes into her face,
And tried to speak but could not. And the while
She marvelled sadly why he seemed so changed,
For in her dream she had not thought of Claude,
But only felt some spell had chained her down
While low and lower still she seemed to fall,
And mocking whispers hissed athwart the gloom,
That she must evermore in darkness dwell.

'Twas late when she awoke. The summer sun
Was shining high, and May, with painful start
And vague remorse, gazed suddenly around,
While Nelly, who had watched her troubled sleep,
Held out to her a note from Blanche Adare.
May took the letter with a trembling hand,

While tears welled slowly in her lustrous eyes,
But flowed not yet—her eyes were as her thoughts,
Too full for motion, and their pearly mist
Remained like sunless dew. Blanche only said,
That she would go as far as Norman-Tower
With Claude that afternoon, and not return
Till late—too late to see her.
                            Few the words,
And closed with fond assurances of love,
Then why was May so sad ? She could not tell—
She felt as sleeping she had dreamed of bliss,
And woke to find it gone. Yet, sooth, it was
The dream that had been sad—for Nell had asked,
" What ailed thee, child ?—why didst thou wail and
        moan
So piteously in sleep ?—I've watched thee long."
 " I ought not to have slept," May simply said,
" For I was happy ere I fell asleep."
Perplexed, the mother mused, yet would not ask
The meaning of this strange reply. In truth,
She could not bear to think that child so loved,
Feared aught of sorrow in her future lot.

PART IV.

THAT morn, ere birds had ceased their matin chants
To slumber in the shade at drowsy noon,
Came Mistress Susan Dean from Dowling's mill
To Nelly's door with quick and joyful steps.
She, Reuben's married sister, had arrived
The day before, from distant country town,
To spend a month with Reuben, see his bride
And Nelly, and attend the marriage feast:
But, being very poor, had only brought
Her youngest babe and dearest, while the rest
Remained in grandam's care.

      "Dear May," quoth she,
" An' thou wilt come this morning to our mill,
My baby take in charge, and mind young Jane,
Then brother Rube will drive me down, he saith,
To see our friends and kin at Norman-Tower."

" I gladly go," said May. But sad at heart
She sallied forth; and yet she strove to feel
Contented, and to crush her strong desire

To see young Claude, if only once, again.
She thought it hard, and somewhat strange, that Blanche
Had written to forbid her coming, since
She said, it was not till the afternoon
That they to Norman-Tower would go. Her mind
Was full of vivid scenes, of pictures fair
Of sweet imaginings of Blanche and Claude.
She saw them in her fancy pace along
The avenue or through the upland glades,
Or haply, linger in the gardens fair,
Where vase-crowned terraces and grassy slopes
Were rising once again as in their prime,
From grim weed-hidden desolation there.
She fancied she could hear their happy tones
As they conversed together; voices sweet
Whose far off echoes in her inmost heart
Had sounded through that blissful wakeful night
Like cadences of music. And she thought
That such a voice, so sweet as Claude Adare's,
Had ever reached her ears before that eve,
Nor would again. She sat beside the cot
And rocked the child to sleep, while Janie read
Aloud her little lesson of small words.

But May could scarcely heed the childish tones;
For where she sat, the casement looked upon
The fair old oaks that bordered Morland Hall;
And oh! if she were only on that hill,
The grassy knoll above that oaken grove,
She could look down and see if Blanche and Claude
Were walking on the terraces below.
She longed to go, if only she could trust
Young Jane to watch the babe while she was gone.
It seemed to sleep so well; it would not wake
For half an hour or more. At last she said,
"Dear Janie, could I trust thee with the child?
Wilt thou take care of baby till he wake?"
And Jane replied, with childlike joy and pride,
"Oh yes, I will; and Auntie Sue has said,
That I am quite a clever little nurse,
And carry Joe as well as she can do."

"Yet, take great care; and mind, if he should wake,
Thou dost not let him toddle out of doors."
"Oh yes, I will take care," said Jane. The child
Was scarcely six years old: but trusted more
Are village children in their early years
Than those of other classes. So May went

And clambered up beneath the spreading trees
To reach the envied height. The path was steep,
Yet soon she gained the summit of the knoll,
And looked straight down upon the Manor House,
And all its gardens glistening in the sun.
Nor Blanche nor Claude were there. It silent lay,
And basking in the noontide glare of June.

  She sat upon the grassy slope and watched,
Hoping that they would soon appear below,
Until the old hall clock struck twelve, and showed
An hour had passed. She started at the sound,
Remembering 'twas the children's dinner hour;
And feared that Janie, wondering why she stayed,
Might with th' impatience of a hungry child
Have left the little one. She started up,
And marvelled where her errant thoughts had been,
In that most swift of hours: then cast one look
Of disappointment at the Hall, and ran
All breathless home. The door stood open wide,
And as she reached it Jane came running out
With countenance perplexed and ill at ease,
As one who is alarmed, yet strives the while
To feel no wrong is done. This May perceived

And asked with trembling voice about the babe.
"Oh, he's quite well," said Janie; "come and look.
He's fast asleep; he did not hear me speak;
He does not hear your step: and yet it's late.
And oh, I am so hungry too."
                        The babe
Was lying still; his eyes were closed, his lips
Were very pale, yet smiled most peacefully.
May looked at him a moment in suspense;
Then stooping down to kiss his little brow,
She started back. "Oh, how is this?" she cried,
"He's cold, quite cold; his clothes are dripping wet."
  "Yes, it's the stream," said Janie; "I went out
To see if you were coming, and the child,
He would come too. I could not keep him back;
He wanted so to see the water shine.
I held his hand quite tight when we were there,
But he would stoop to look, and tried to catch
The other little boy he saw in it,
And then he slipped away from me and fell.
I could not stop him; down the bank he rolled,
But I went in at once and pulled him out.
He did not speak, for he was fast asleep;

So gently in the cot I laid him down,
And he has slept quite quiet ever since."

  Poor May had seen death once. Old Jonas looked
E'en so, but he was old. This could not be.
Oh no, it could not be the child was dead !
She caught him up, and shrieked with fear and woe,
Then ran with him all down the village street,
And never stopped for breath until she reached
Old Nelly's door.

              'Twas true! The child was drowned.

PART V.

THROUGH many sleepless nights and weary days
  Did Nelly watch beside her, fearing much
That now the happy years of May's young life
Were drawing to their close. And Blanche Adare
Sat oft beside the sufferer's bed, and strove
To comfort Reuben, and speak cheering words
Of hope to all. To Susan Dean, whose grief
Had filled the measure of the self-reproach
That haunted May, she sent, with kindly words,
Most costly gifts for all her little ones,
And presents for her husband and herself;
Not unacceptable—for unto those
Whose lot it is to earn with daily care
A bare subsistence equal to their needs,
If grief be e'er so deep, a few kind gifts,
And kinder words, avail to comfort much.

  But Reuben—reasoning little, feeling much—
Had grown meanwhile, his purpose to renounce
Concerning May: convinced that, should she live,

He ne'er could make her happy. True it is
That Love divines where Reason is at fault:
And simple rustic natures have a sense
More quick than reason; such can oft descry
The germ of ill, the hidden cause of grief
In those they love. How oft an aged nurse
Divines the motives hid 'neath smiles or tears,
That actuate for evil or for good
The children of her care! 'Twas so with him.

  Though nought he knew concerning Claude, nor knew
That sight of him had puzzled May's young heart,
(As magnet doth the trembling needle draw
From her allegiance to the frozen pole,)
Yet he divined the hidden grief that sucked
The roses from her cheeks; and as, in sooth,
He felt more clearly than he could reflect,
He was by feeling, not reflection, led.

  Oft he recalled to mind how she had looked
Before and since the wedding day was named;
And he compared the child-like trust she showed,
With the impassioned gladsome light that shone
In Jane's dark eyes, his first and loving wife,

When he had woo'd and won her maiden heart;
How fitful blushes mantled in her cheeks,
And how they came and went at his approach;
And how her eyes would shine: she once had said
His steps were set to music—she who now
Reposed beneath the daisies peacefully.

But May had looked both shy and grave, nay, sad,
Since they had been betrothed, and seemed oppressed
With unelastic weight of care that pressed
Her gentle spirit down. And thus it was,
That after much long commune with himself—
Thoughts without words, and feelings without thought,
He came to his resolve. He begged his aunt
To tell poor May when she could comprehend,
(For yet her mind oft wandered painfully),
To tell her even midst her ravings wild,
Rather than not at all—such was his prayer—
That he had quite released her from her troth.
He hoped it might revive her sinking heart
To feel herself unfettered, free to choose
Her lot in life.
   They told her these his words
One evening, when they thought she seemed more calm,

And, for a moment, Blanche could plainly see
A look of joy flit o'er her pale thin face;
But soon 'twas gone, and with a steady voice
She said, "I know why Reuben wishes this.
He thinks I love him not: but 'tis not so;
For I have inly vowed that I will strive
Much more than erst, (if God doth spare my life),
To make him happy. Ask him to forgive
My awful sin that caused the dear babe's death,
That so, I living yet awhile, may bring
A little joy to him deserving much."

Blanche saw the effort, and admiring, loved
The maiden more than ever, and expressed
Her confidence that May would find all joys
Grow up and blossom round the path in life
Which she had wisely chosen. But the dame
Desponding, shook her head at this advice,
And guided by the instinct that instructs
The pure uneducated mind, agreed
With Reuben and approved of his resolve.

This May perceived, and asked persistently
That he be sent for. So he came in haste;

And then she prayed him to forgive her sin,
And let her try to bring him happiness.

He, seeing that her wearied mind was bent
On this intention quite exclusively,
With tact of true affection, nothing said
Against her wishes; but he kissed her hand,
And marked with grief how great the contrast showed
Between its lily fairness and his brown
Work hardened, roughly shapen palm. Again
He inly vowed, that never, never more—
Or not, at least, until long years had passed—
Would he behold that sweetest face again,
Convinced that she had plighted him her troth
To please old Nelly Rolfe and not herself.

That day when Reuben left her, sorrowing
He passed the open portal of the church,
For 'twas a saint's day, and, the service done,
The sextoness had left the door ajar
For sunshine to steal in, and drive away
The clammy vapours foul and stagnant air,
Which in our parish churches now supply
The place of incense and of ceaseless prayers.

He paused a moment; then he entered in,

And humbly knelt beside the altar rails.
This was the month, and this the very place,
Where he had hoped to claim his bride ; but, no,
He would not think of that—he only wished
To pray for guidance now, and light to see
How best he might insure her happiness,
And give her no just cause for self-reproach.
For this he prayed, and then with strength arose
To carry out a plan—quite sudden now—
Yet formed three years before, when he had erst
Begun to love the beauteous May too well.
He would depart from England, take his child,
And, with her, all the hoarding of his life
And produce of his farm, to seek a home
Where, rising in the southern sea, an isle,
Shining with sands of gold, bids fair to prove
Another England in far future times,
When we shall all be dust. There he would go,
And speedily : it was the only way
To free the timorous conscience of his love.
For months she should not know where he was gone ;
He would divide him from her by the sea.
To Nell alone would he confide his plans

And purposes, that when three years had passed,
If May were still unwedded, and should wish
Till then as now she wished, he would return
And end his days with her, his bride beloved,
If God so willed it, in his native vale.
Thus Reuben went, and with such skilful speed
His plans, matured in wakeful nights, were formed,
That none but Nelly guessed where he had gone,
Nor was it known till many months had passed,
What far off land had claimed him for her own.

PART VI.

FIVE weeks had fled, when from the Viscount came
　　A letter to his daughter. It announced
His speedy coming, and his wish declared
To take her with him northwards. Sad and brief,
And selfish were his words. He seemed to care
But little for the beauties of the vale,
But little for the Manor House, and yet
His restless spirit had been bent erewhile
On its adornment. Blanche, too, felt sad,
And marvelled at his mood, till musing on't,
She apprehended sorrows yet unknown,
Not taking shape and circumstances, but vague
As waking nightmares. She had learned to love
The quaint old Manor House of bygone times
Far better than their grander northern home,
Where e'en in childhood she had grown to feel
How little grandeur adds to happiness.
For oft her father seemed to be a prey
To agony of mind. Reports had reached

Her ears, when quite a child, that he had done
Some fearful wrong, yet what, she never knew.

   Strange words are whispered low in nurseries,
Nor meant to reach the little children's ears,
Supposed to be in peaceful slumbers locked,
Or deemed, perchance, too young to comprehend
The meaning of their elders. But, the while,
Such vague mysterious hints by nurses dropped,
Uncomprehended at the time, sink deep
Into the children's quickened wondering ears,
And long years afterwards are understood.

   Blanche loved her sire: for though to all beside,
Stern, haughty, and repellent he appeared,
To her and Claude he had been ever kind—
Yet not a tender nor a careful parent;
This she felt, but scarcely would confess,
Nor ever could endure to hear him blamed.

   Few friends had Blanche, she was by nature shy,
And had from childhood lived so much alone.
Her father shunned his neighbours—nay, perchance
He had been shunned by them—she knew not which,
Nor ever had she sought companionship
Except her brother Claude's, till May she found.

The maiden's lovely face, as by the porch
She stood on that glad eve when Blanche first came,
Reminded her of some one, with a strange
Yet joyous sense of mystery—of some
Fair picture she had seen; or else, perchance,
Some dream that she had dreamed. And this had first
Attracted her; then, rumours that she heard,
Awoke those recollections of her youth
Long dormant, of a time long, long ago,
When mingled joy and woe had seemed more keen
Than in her after years. Yes, she had seen
In bygone times some beauteous face like May's.

'Twas not her mother's portrait—she had died
When Blanche was born. It was a fairer face,
With beaming eyes, arched eyebrows, and the same
Profusion of a sunset-tinted hair,
Curling around a snowy swan-like throat.
'Twas surely not a dream. The nurses, too,
Had whispered of a lady wondrous fair:
They said, "Ah, well, she will not suffer more;
Her bed is quiet, and the marble slabs
Are doors not quickly opened. 'Tis as well;

One can't be murdered more than once, and life
Is sad enough."
    "But, what of him, my Lord?"
"He knows a deal more than you think he does"—
"Lord, bless you, how he loved her."
        " Yet, 'twas he
As sure as fate who did it, and 'twill out;
Yes, mark my words, 'twill out when we are dust,
When we are dust and worms, if not before.
Why, look at him, you'll see it in his face."
 "Hush, there's that child, we wake her with our
   talk:
Come down to supper."
      Each strange word and tone
Had Blanche remembered through her after life.
At times she thought 'twas some delirious dream
Of fever born, which might have ta'en such shape
Of horror and of dread. For how could he,
Her father, e'er have murdered one he loved?
It was too horrible. "'Tis hate alone;
'Tis hate, not love, that kills," repeated she.
Yet haunting fears from childhood's days derived,

When thus the nurses darkly talked together,
Now appeared to grow in ghastly shape.
　And all these recollections, though indeed
So fraught with pain, seemed but to draw her more
With an attraction irresistible
And strange to Nelly's child.
　　　　　　　　　Blanche dearly loved
The gentle girl, and gladly would have done,
Nay, suffered much for her, if this could win
The child's true happiness; and much she grieved
To leave her, too, in leaving Morland Hall.
She thought her fitted well to grace a throne,
Yet, viewing all the risks and ills of life,
And perils many, she could see for her
No better lot than Reuben's bride to be.
A like impression May had made on Claude:
He felt a glad surprise at sight of her,
As at a dream fulfilled. And yet a dread,
Vague, undefined, oppressed him; caused, perchance,
By just the same surmise that troubled Blanche,
Though never had he spoken on't to her,
Nor she to him. Blanche saw, indeed, that May
Embodied, as it were, his purest dreams,

And that her image had been graven deep,
Too deep, perchance, on his impassioned heart,
For after he had gone, she found a sketch
Traced by his hand, as he had seen her first,
On entering his sister's western room.
The sunset aureole round her shining head,
Her lily face in glowing shade, her eyes
Half hid beneath their lashes' silken fringe,
And hastily beneath these words were traced:—

   "Just so, some beauteous saint in storied glass,
   Where ceaseless chants in dim cathedrals rise,
   Transmits the light of heaven, and seems to give,
   Its glory, tempered for our sin-dimmed eyes.

   "Oh! may this image come before my soul
   In after years; when weary from the strife,
   In some enchanted island, I may find
   Temptation to forget the better life.

   "Yes, weary from the strife—for earth appears
   A tear-stained battle-field where all must die;
   Where banners, laurel-wreaths, and golden crowns,
   With those who fought for them, down-trodden lie.

"And yet, methinks, I feel a soft reproach,
  For gloomy thoughts beam from those eyes so fair;
  Sweet saint, not only from the syren's wiles
  Protect, but lure me too from dark despair."

She told him then, by letter, how poor May
Had nearly died of grief at having caused
The death of Susan's babe. Blanche never knew
The cause of May's unwonted negligence,
For Nell had prayed her not to ask, had said
That May when questioned on't had swooned with grief,
Nor woke, save 'mid delirious ravings wild,
That had betrayed to Nell some hidden woe;
So Blanche suspected not that Claude Adare
Might have impressed the youthful heart of May
With more than the esteem which she must feel
For one whose praises she had often heard.
And May, by eager impulse often led,
With undeveloped power and genius filled,
Susceptible deep impress to receive
Of all that fired her young enthusiasm,
Was so unlike herself, that scarce could Blanche

Follow the sudden changes of her mind,
Or comprehend its wild imaginings.

   July was near its close, and May as yet
Had never left the house, and scarce her room;
But one bright morn she felt a sudden strength,
And longing irresistible to walk
As far as Morland Hall. "I wish," she said,
" Once more to see it, ere my Lady Blanche
Doth leave it for so long." She felt, that then
To visit its deserted silent rooms,
Would be a trial greater than her strength.
   Besides, the sketch—the sketch she had begun,
Which Claude had praised—was left there, and she
      wished
To have it, although inwardly resolved
To think of none but Reuben, and to wait
Until he should return to claim his bride.
   Nell shook her head disprovingly, and said,
" Thou art not strong enough to walk so far;"
Yet thankful that her child could frame such wish,
The Dame went forth with her, until they reached
The avenue, and there met Blanche herself.

On seeing them she was at first o'erjoyed,
But when they closer came, and she could mark
The ravages by illness made on May,
The cheek so pale and thin, the weary walk,
More visible by far than in the house,
She could have wept for grief. But she concealed
Her apprehension 'neath a prudent smile,
Then helped the maiden's steps with loving care,
And led her to the oriel that she loved.

And there they passed the day. The summer air
Came softly sighing through the casement wide,
And bore the orange blossoms' odour sweet,
From vases on the terraces beneath.
A golden mist hung o'er the distant downs
And o'er the purple woods. The Abbey towers,
Athwart the haze in greater grandeur loomed,
Each mullioned tracery in light defined.
And, 'mid the waving foliage of the oaks,
That stretched their loving arms across its banks,
The river glided, darting shafts of light,
As through the vale it wound and passed away.

And May looked happy, and she seemed to grow
More strong with each succeeding sunny hour,

As if resolved all care to cast aside
For this one day. And when the summer clouds,
Like courtiers, ranged themselves in straight long
    lines,
Attired in crimson and in gold, to wait
Their mighty monarch's exit through the west,
The portals of the sunset, she prepared
To bid a long adieu to Morland Hall,
Resolving not to visit it again
Until some happy day months hence, when Blanche
Should come again. Most beautiful she looked:
The setting sunbeams kissed her golden hair,
And tinged with roseate hue her lily cheek;
Her deep blue eyes were fixed on Blanche with love
Intensified in this their parting hour.
And so absorbed was Blanche, rejoiced to see
Her friend so beautiful, and e'en to mark
A visible improvement since the morn,
She did not hear a footstep on the stairs,
Nor see the door had opened, till a voice,
Or rather moaning cry of one in pain,
Had reached her ear. Then, starting round, she saw

Her father there—but so unlike himself
She scarcely recognized him. Upon May
His staring eyes were fixed, and with a gaze
Of horror mingled with a wild delight,
As if the vision from the spirit world
Of one long lost and mourned, before him stood.
He noted not his daughter's presence there,
His thoughts were riveted on May alone.
Thus fixed his gaze remained, while o'er his face
Strange passions chased each other, like the clouds
On windy moonlit nights, till Blanche perceived
A deadly pallor overspread his face
The while with palsied lips he tried to speak—
Then sank upon a chair, and, shuddering, pressed
His hands upon his eyes. "Who, who is this?"
He said, "I must be dreaming. Tell me who?"
But Blanche led May affrighted from the room,
And strove some plausible excuse to give
For such strange anguish on her father's face;
Then hastened back to him. The dreaded ill
Seemed certainly at hand. Her father's guilt,
By hints infused into her childish mind

In days when nurses whispered to each other,
Now a shape more tangible assumed.

  She found him still in the same attitude
Of woe and shame ; but, as she nearer came,
His head sank backwards slowly, and a cry
As if of one in mortal agony
Struck on her ears. And then she saw him fall
Insensible upon the marble hearth.
Her people summoned by her piercing cries,
Helped her to raise him up, and in their arms
They bore him to his bed, while messengers
Were sent to summon Claude.

                      A weary hour
Of dread suspense his daughter passed, while May
Was wondering in alarm and grief, if she
By some strange accident had caused this woe.
She longed to be of use, but Blanche, with tears
And warm caress, implored her to begone,
Then added, 'mid impassioned words of love,
" Go, for he likes not strangers, that is all.
But if he can his health regain, I know
A day will come when he will love you well.
Ah! he deserves your pity and your prayers.

Now, go, my child speak not, lest he perchance
Should hear your voice. But ask Dame Rolfe to come
And help to nurse my father through the night."

PART VII.

SOME nineteen years before, Lord Hollingbourne,
  Then Hugh Adare, an only son, had been
Involved in debts; the sharp and sour fruits
Of reckless youth. His fair young wife, oppressed
With days of care and nights of dread, expired
'Mid winter snows, in giving birth to Blanche,
The youngest of their children. Then were left
The motherless, to struggle on alone
As best they might, for Hugh fled o'er the sea
For greater safety. And he chanced to see
At Brussels, tarrying with some relatives,
A maiden fair, called Geraldine O'Neil,
Her mother was the Geraldine Adare,
Whom Nelly Rolfe had nursed and loved so well—
And who had married Everard O'Neil,
The colonel of an Indian regiment.
She lived but two short years; then brave O'Neil,
The broken-hearted, fell an easy prey
To fever nurtured 'neath that torrid sun,

And thus their orphan child was left; the last,
The last remaining of that ancient race
Who had for many generations dwelt
In Morland's happy vale.

                        Fair Geraldine!
All Brussels talked of her: the English girl
With sunset-tinted hair, and wondrous eyes,
And called her, in their homage, Dawn of Day.
Her troth was plighted to Lord Hollingbourne,
Hugh's cousin, then a soldier, and in Spain,
But soon expected thence.

                      Oh, Love! most blind,
Misleading him of heavenly guidance reft,
With semblance of an angel, into dark
And tortuous paths of sin, and yet the while
An angel truly to the pure in heart:
From paradisal gardens wafting down
Life-giving odours from thy snowy wings,
Thou com'st to man a Blessing or a Curse.
A curse to him enslaved by love of self,
A joy to him through love of God made free,
To that—a fatuous light amid a swamp,
To this—the sunrise o'er a seething sea.

LADY MAY.

An evil angel in a shape of light,
Love came 'mid sorrow's night to Hugh Adare;
Came like a gleam of purest light from heaven,
Upon the swamps and quicksands of his life,
Luring him on to greater depths of woe,
And recklessly he followed.
      When he saw
Fair Geraldine O'Neil, the orphan girl,
(To see her was to love her,) he resolved
That she should be his Dawn of Day, nor cared
If treason to his cousin were involved
In such mad vows. But gentle Geraldine
Despised his suit, his talents, and his wit;
His fascination, that men babbled of,
Appeared to her deformity; she scorned
The want of purpose which she felt, not saw,
The vaunted beauty which she saw, not felt,
And to him closed her doors and maiden heart.
 Then, mad with rage, he plotted and contrived,
How best t' instil into his cousin's mind
Distrust of his betrothed. But vain such arts,
The simple trust and purity of both
Were proof against his utmost wit and wile,

For they, without suspecting Hugh, surmised
That traitorous hand was plotting 'gainst their weal,
And smiling, closer to each other clung.
'Tis ever thus, the citadel must show
Some weaker point ere vanquished by the foe;
A scorpion strikes not through the coat of mail,
And limpid waters check the poisoned gale.

So they were married, Viscount Hollingbourne
And Geraldine, but on their wedding day,
Clash of opposing arms was almost heard
In many-spirèd Brussels. Brief their joy,
For ere three suns had set and risen, he,
The bridegroom, to the battle-field was called,
And Geraldine well nigh of anguish died,
So sure she felt they ne'er should meet again
In this sad world. But he, a better hope
Strove to impart, and kissed away her tears,
Yet made his will, bequeathing all his wealth
And properties to her if he should die.

Th' opposing armies met: a glorious day
For bleeding Europe, and for England's fame,
But fatal to so many of her sons

Who offered priceless holocausts of life,
And youth, and hope, to purchase victory.

   Among the bravest of the brave that day,
And foremost in the fight, was Hollingbourne.
He lived to see it won, but, wounded sore,
He sank, and at the sunset hour he died.

   No need of messenger to tell his loss!
For at that self-same hour poor Geraldine
Had ceased to hope. The sad presentiment,
Which ever since he went possessed her heart,
Assumed a shape more tangible: she thought
His dying eyes gazed with a glorious light
In her's, and seemed to look a last farewell;
And then she heard him most distinctly say,
"Take heart, sweet love; soon shall we meet again
In happiness eternal and complete."

PART VIII.

NO sooner did the fatal news arrive,
　Than Hugh assumed the title, and laid claim
To all the properties therewith entailed,
And thus belonging rightfully to him,
In failure of his cousin's lawful heir.
By will, Lord Hollingbourne could but dispose
In favour of his widow, of those lands
Which from his mother were derived. But these
Were passing large, so Geraldine was rich,
Though nought she cared for wealth, nor had a wish,
Except on earth to serve her God, and soon
Rejoin the husband she so deeply loved,
In happiness eternal and complete.
Few friends had she, and none to care that Hugh
Had thus assumed the title, ere full time
Had passed in which an heir might possibly
Be born. The barony, in Edward's reign
Bestowed upon Adares for fealty
And service well performed in border wars,

Descended to the females of their line,
Although the modern visconty belonged
To males alone. But all their large estates
Were with the ancient barony entailed;
So, if the viscountess should prove with child
Of either sex, her offspring would have right
To all its father's fortune and estates.
And this the present viscount knew right well,
Yet took advice from one a so-called friend,
A worthless wretch, whose interest in him
Proceeded from the hope of selfish gains.
" For," said the tempter, " if Hugh's debts were paid,
Himself thus free to watch o'er Geraldine,
And act as guardian should a child be born,
'Twere best for her." And so, with pretext fair,
Of watching o'er the widow's wealth, Hugh came
To England's shores, and soon, by wily means,
Contrived to assume control o'er all her lands,
As well as those entailed upon the title.

Geraldine, meanwhile, had much desired
To see her husband's castle, Norman-Tower,
And thither she arrived, although o'erwhelmed
With loneliness and woe. His kindred all,

Were dead or far away, and knew her not,
But much she loved to see what he had loved,
The objects that his eyes had rested on,
As were his glance o'erfraught with harmony
That lingered round them still. She loved to trace
His likeness in ancestral portraits; through
Fair woods to roam, which he had oft described,
And glades where he had chased the fallow-deer;
In summer evenings linger on the lake,
Or saunter in the gardens he had loved,
And list while aged servitors would tell
Unnumbered histories of his gracious youth.
So months passed on, and then a hope so blessed
Began to dawn, that e'en she wept for joy!
A child! her dearest Arthur's child and her's,
Would soon be born. But could she hope to rear
The babe, if living? Grief had undermined
Her strength and health; so of necessity
She must a just and upright guardian seek,
Who would protect the babe.
      Full long she mused,
Then suddenly she thought of John O'Neil,
Her father's brother. Straight she wrote to him;

Implored his presence, and with cautious hints
Endeavoured to express that Hollingbourne
Was not a man to whom she could entrust
The welfare of her child.   No answer came.
She wrote again and yet again, and watched
With grief and wonder; still came no reply.
Meanwhile from Hugh a missive had arrived,
Proving his wondrous interest in her fate.
With words of tender comfort, yet subdued,
He said her Yorkshire lands had been involved
In such confusion by a worthless steward
That worlds of trouble he had ta'en to place
The property in order, and he hoped
She soon would come to see what he had done.

   That he was far away consoled her most,
For great her dread had been lest he should come
To Norman-Tower, where no sure refuge she
From his most baneful presence could devise.

   The English nurse she had of late engaged
Was daughter to a servant of the house,
And married to the gamekeeper, who came
But lately to the place.   And Geraldine
His face misliked, yet half reproached herself

For such mistrust, since all spoke well of him ;
And with a kind of penitence she heaped
Favours upon him for his good wife's sake.
A buxom dame she was ; most trusty seemed,
And spoke with fitting tenderness and love
Of Geraldine's lamented lord, while words
Of disrespect, made pungent by dislike,
She lavished upon Hugh.

      "My lord ! indeed !"
She said with tossing head and curling lip ;
" No right to claim the title and estates
Has he : and he'll be finely taken in
When our dear babe is born."

       Week followed week
While Geraldine was waiting nervously ;
Still had no letter come from John O'Neil,
Or promise of his coming. And one day
At even, faintness seized her suddenly ;
Then dreading lest the trial hour had come
So much too soon, she told her nurse to send
In haste for a physician. None arrived ;
And whether in much nervousness, the nurse
Forgot her lady's bidding, or her words

Misunderstood, nay heard not, none could tell :
'Twas only known that dawn had chased the night,
Long hours had passed before the groom was sent;
And ere the echoes of his horse's hoofs
Had ceased to ring beneath the castle gates,
Fair Geraldine's pure soul had ta'en its flight
And found a Dawn of Day more bright than our's.
Then were the inmates of the castle told
That she had suddenly, in fainting, died ;
That no child had been born. That self-same eve,
When the physician hurriedly arrived,
He found the viscount kneeling near her bed,
With all the outward signs of grief immense,
Deploring that he had arrived too late
To see his much loved cousin ere she died.
Within that silent room they tarried long,
The doctor and Lord Hollingbourne, where lay
The lifeless form of Geraldine Adare ;
But what between them passed was never known.
   Two suns arose and set, and then they bore
Her sable coffin to the marble vaults,
While marvelled all the servitors at such
(For so they deemed it) strange unseemly haste.

And e'er a month had passed the buxom nurse
Of fever died with ravings dread to hear,
Then straight the gamekeeper, her husband, went
And ne'er returned.   Lord Hollingbourne appeared
Henceforth to loathe the wealth that he had gained.
Deserted was the castle: never more
He visited the place; nor was he heard
To name its name: but travelled quickly north
And in his Yorkshire dwelling fixed his home.

There in all solitary state he lived,
And reared his children, whom he jealous kept
From converse with their fellows; he, the while
Ne'er seen to smile, but shunning all his friends:
While whisperings mysterious and dark hints
Among the nursemaids and retainers gnawed,
Like rats, his children's confidence away,
And left them hearts half emptied of his love.

PART IX.

Pale Blanche sat watching by her father's bed,
The night when he arrived at Morland Hall.
No words his dry lips passed; but piteous moans
At intervals she heard. The doctor came;
It chanced to be the same who years before
Arrived too late at Norman-Tower to see
The lonely widow die. He had not met
Lord Hollingbourne since.

"My lord is changed;
Ah! greatly changed," he whispered low to Blanche;
"I scarce should know him for the same. He owned
A constitution fitted well to last
A century. Some sudden shock was this?"
Blanche led him from the room, then faltering said,
"He was excited strangely here this night,
When May, a village girl, he saw. Her face
May some resemblance bear to one, perchance,
Whom he had known and loved."

"A likeness; well,"
The doctor said, "that surely is no cause:
The fit must have been coming on. You said
He unexpected came. It was the heat;
Or the too rapid journey." "True," said Blanche,
Relieved to think her father's malady
Might come from other cause than sight of May.
Then she returned with better heart to watch
Beside his bed. The danger for his life
Was great, the doctor had confessed, and said
They were to call him if a change occurred,
Then went to bed and slept.
                              Old Nelly Rolfe
Had come to Morland Hall and sat by Blanche,
Keeping throughout that night her wakeful watch,
Oblivious of fatigue. It was enough
That he who lay in such extremity
Her services required; it was enough
That still he bore the name she loved so well.

  The moonbeams through the mullioned window shone
Upon the polished floor and wainscot wall;
And Nelly looked around with awe, for this—
This was the room where Geraldine was born.

LADY MAY.

As then, so now, it was a moonlight night,
The pale and ghostly beams assumed the shape
Of gothic arches on the oaken floor,
And now, as then, amid their silver light,
The mullioned transom formed a shadowy cross.
'Twas more than sixty years ago since Nell,
A girl of fifteen summers, had kept watch
Beside the nurse, while slept a painful sleep
The lady of the hall. Aye, since that night
Full sixty-five long years had passed. The room
Was scarcely changed. She well-nigh could have thought
Her life since then had been one long strange dream;
That still she watched beside her lady's couch,
While near her lay young Geraldine, a child
So dear, she thought her birth must surely bring
Some blessing to the house. As thus she mused
The moonbeams slowly crept along the floor,
The cross in shadow reached the bed, and then
It touched the sufferer's stiff and pallid hands
Where on the broidered coverlet they lay.
Though Nelly's gaze upon those hands was fixed,
She scarce their movement saw, so deep she mused,
Nor marked the chain of gold they clutched, and how

They strove to hide a something at its end.
But Blanche, more watchful, sought with straining eyes
The secret of her father's life to read.
The cross in shadow and the moonbeams crept
Still higher up, and touched his troubled brow.
Perchance the light disturbed him, for he moved,
He started as in greater pain, and raised
His clenched hand suddenly, then loosed its grasp,
And from it fell an oval miniature.
The golden rim bright glistened in the light,
Depicted there Nell saw a well-known face,
A face like May's; but ah! resembling more
Her own beloved lost Geraldine. Blanche saw,
Remembered too. In happier hours of childhood,
When her sire had with her played, at times
He would uplift her, place her on his knee,
Then hold that miniature before her eyes
And let her kiss it, then approving smiled
As if the sight of it possessed a charm
To soothe the rugged fierceness of his mind.

But only in her very earliest days
Could this have happened, so remote and dim
The time appeared. And then it must have ceased;

For she remembered nought in after years,
Save a faint consciousness of past delight,
And yearning for it. Then she saw young May,
And wondered: now the miniature itself
Supplied the missing link in memory's chain,
That bound the maiden to a happy past.
Yes, strangely happy—although mixed with dread,
A dread that hourly grew through reasoning on't,
And seeing how her father's dying grasp
Thus jealous, had the miniature concealed.
 At early dawn of day he seemed to rest
As if he suffered less. And suddenly
His eyes were opened, and he looked at Blanche,
Then recognised her, and in haste he clutched,
As if he would conceal, the miniature:
"I've had a dream," he said with feeble voice,
"A fearful, yet a very happy dream."
But, seeing Nelly, added, "Who is this?
Where am I, Blanche? I thought I saw her face,
The Dawn of Day. But first dismiss that woman:
I would speak a word with you alone."
Nell gave restoratives, and prayed that he

Would rest awhile to gain some needful strength
Ere yet he tried to speak; then left the room.

   And much she hoped he would confess the sin
That made his dying hours so full of pain.
Accustomed through her long and useful life
To see men die, she well had learned to know
The evil signs of guilt which darkly haunt
The dying sinner's bed. And all that night
The viscount's troubled face told more of pain
Occasioned by a conscience ill at ease
Than anguish of the body.

                       Patiently
She knelt beside his chamber door and prayed.
The sun had risen, and its cheering ray
Illumed the eastern window pane, which bore
The old heraldic shield of the Adares.
Still gleamed the colours vivid as of yore,
And while she kneeling humbly prayed for him
Who lay there dying, and a blessing craved
For May and Blanche, the well known silver cross
On blood-red shield shone o'er her folded hands
A cross in light. Full-joyfully she hailed

The dazzling emblem of salvation there,
Which seemed to bless her prayers.

                        And what of him,
Lord Hollingbourne? He lay a dying now,
And all was dark before his troubled gaze;
No light had he been taught to see beyond
The portals of this fast receding world.
The lowly dame who knelt beside his door
Was older far than he, her eyes were dim,
Her ears were dull of hearing, but the cross,
The cross in shadow meekly borne at first
Had turned to one of radiance pure and bright,
That all her soul illumined. Hallowed thoughts
Consoled her, such as fill the minds of those
Who steadfast teach themselves to love the good,
Who find more beauty in the sparkling dew
That glistens on a single blade of grass
Than gleam of priceless pearl or diamond
In regal crown. Those who have suffered much,
And have their cross resignedly embraced,
Will surely find that these their kisses pure,
Bestowed on it, will at the last transform
Its painful shade into a brilliant light

Shining with radiance from within o'er all
The present and the past, and brighter joy
Conferring on the dim and sightless eyes
Than fairest object to the gaze of youth.

 Oh dread not age, if young thou keep'st thy heart;
'Tis only on the old in sin, on those
Whom age despise, that age inflicts despair,
And malady of soul than death more dread.

 Meanwhile, with straining ear Blanche listened keen
To catch the utterance of her father's words.
"Whose was the form," he said, "and whose the face
I saw erewhile? 'Twas surely not a dream?"

 "Nay, 'twas a village girl; a little maid,"
Said Blanche, with cautious words, "who oft has come
To cheer my solitude."

     "Deceive me not,"
He said with trembling irritated voice;
"Her parentage is other than you say."

 "Indeed, I know not," faltered Blanche, "perhaps
It may be so. Old Nelly Rolfe, the nurse,
Discovered her, a babe just newly born,
Nigh eighteen years ago, in Quarry Wood,
Suspended in a rosebush o'er the dark

And silent waters of the High Oak Pond.
Above it runs the old highroad that leads
To Norman-Tower; beneath, the deep mill stream
That through the valley winds."

"It must," he cried,
"It must then be her child! Oh Geraldine!
Forgive, forgive my treachery. How oft,
When dark and cruel shadows through the night
Of all these weary years, have made my rest
Less restful than the ploughman's toilsome days,
How often have I thought that I would give
All, all the loathsome wealth that I have gained,
And even face disgrace and obloquy
If thy babe's life could be restored. For this
I've almost tried to pray. O hear me now,
And pardon, God of sinners! Let me give,
O let me give her back her lands, her name!
O let me feel that I have pardon gained,
By this dear token, finding her at last,
Unhoped for, thricely welcomed, mourned so long,
Aye, mourned as never child before was wept!
With all a father's anguish of despair,
Who loved her mother more than life itself;

With all a sinner's anguish of remorse,
Who for a score of years, with bleeding feet
Hath toiled along life's sharp and flinty path.
Send for her quickly; let me trace again
The lineaments belovèd. Bring the nurse,
That she may prove thy words. Yet stay, my child,
(Thou wilt not hate thy father?) let me tell
The miserable story ere I die.
'Tis growing dark : come closer; bring more lights."

His head sank back; his forehead pale, bedewed
With drops of mental anguish, weeping Blanche
Refreshed with odours cool and sweet, and kissed
His pallid hands, and raised him in her arms
Until the sunlight shone upon his face,
And then he smiled.

      "She pardons me," he said;
" And justice will be done to her at last !"
" My father, rest awhile," entreated Blanche ;
" Sleep, and beside thee I will watch."

         "No, no ;
But listen. I am better now; and time
Is very precious. It was long ago :—
I listened to a menial in my pay,

A confidential wretch who knew too much,
And used that knowledge glibly. He it was,
Who, covetous of profit, bade me seize
That portion of my cousin's wealth, by right
Mine own, entailed upon the next of kin,
If haply he no lawful heir should leave.
I did so, and my pressing debts discharged.
Thus able to return, I hoped to live
Upon the property, and there atone
By prudence and good management for all
The follies of my youth. I long had loved
With fiery passionate absorbing love,
My cousin's widow, Geraldine Adare.
Oh! could I but have seen her, ere she knew
The viscount, and was taught to hate my name!
No, not by him; I wrong him even now.
O wretch that I have been! I will not seek
My madness to excuse: and yet for her
My love was pure; the only influence
That drew me upwards all those weary years.
Weary and profitless! yet how I wronged
That gentle soul; for, hounded on by him,
This scoundrel Jacob, who an influence gained

O'er all my actions, by a foolish deed
To him, alas! well known, I murdered her.
Nay, shrink not: not by poison or cold steel,
But by a deed of cruelty, which sapped
Her tender life away. I see it now.
O frightful punishment for foulest plot!
He, Jacob, shewed me that if any heir
Were born and lived, not only should I lose
The properties and lands, but should be forced
To render up account of moneys spent,
And thus disclose the evil I had done.
Disgraced, I should be forced to fly again,
Be banished from her presence evermore,
Nor dare, thus branded with new obloquy,
To hope in time her priceless love to win.
Such dread alternative decided me.
Such misery was not to be endured;
And so I let him foully plot and plan
Against the life of the expected babe.
He soon contrived to place his wife as nurse
At Norman-Tower, as gamekeeper himself;
And trusted much by Lady Hollingbourne,
Spies on her every action they became.

They intercepted letters sent by her,
And handed them to me: the while she pined,
Because the time of birth drew near, and yet
No friend or guardian came to her. Alas!
I—I was there at hand—in Jacob's lodge
Concealed, and waiting till the child be born.
So well he managed that not e'en his wife
Suspected that he meant the baby ill;
She only thought I wished to bring it up
As if it were my own, with care and love.
So off he rode upon the swiftest steed,
Bearing the babe. It was the eighth of May;
At dawn I stood below the northern tower,
Where secretly I had been waiting long,
And hoping for good news of Geraldine.
I knew that Jacob with the babe had gone;
For I had seen him creeping stealthily
Beneath the shadow of the eastern wall.
No words he said: I scarcely dared to look,
But well I knew the babe was in his arms.
A weary hour passed on; then came the nurse,
Frantic, scarce knowing what she did, and cried
That all was over, and the mother dead!

Dead! Geraldine! I reeling staggered back,
But, mastering my agony, rushed up
Through winding turret stairs, through corridors
And galleries, until I reached her room.
'Twas true; my torment had begun. She lay
So calm and peaceful, 'twas as if she slept.
I scarcely dared to look upon her face,
So hallowed, yet so wondrous lovely still:
Yet there I lingered. I had murdered her!
The only being I had ever loved.
Her death, so unexpected, drove me mad:
For I reproached the nurse with bitter words,
And asked her fiercely for the babe, and she
Weeping and wailing, solemnly declared
That Geraldine had never known its loss;
For at its birth she sank, and fainting died.
But often I have felt convinced since then
That the poor mother had lived long enough
To see—to feel her baby torn away,
Then of such grief expired. And this through me!
'Twas I who caused it: 'twas my cruelty
That brought her to her grave—the beauteous one,
In youth's first bloom—and left me desolate.

My fell ambition had defeated love,
And thus o'erleapt itself. For I had hoped
That when some years had passed, she might have
        learned
To love me: worthless save in loving her!
That I with true devotion might wash out
The stains of my enforcèd treachery;
For so I deemed it then. How deep my woe!
How deep: the while some thought it was assumed.
Assumed! Ah, yes; my right hand I had given
To purchase such assumption; such amount
Of innocence compared with this my guilt.
The doctor came, though afterwards the nurse
Confessed he was not called till all was o'er.
He found me there beside her lifeless form,
So overwhelmed with grief he ne'er could think
That I had done her wrong. I raved with words
Impassioned, of her virtues, loveliness,
And boundless charm, then hurried him away;
And saying that 'twould drive me mad to wait
About that cursèd dwelling, straight ordained
A hasty funeral. And ne'er did he
Suspect, nor any in the castle think

That she had borne a child. Except the nurse
None guessed the hideous truth. She, clamorous,
Deplored with tears her lady's death, and said
'Twas caused by sudden fainting fits; that such
Had oft been wont to seize her, but had passed,
And that so lengthened and severe was none
As this which ended but with life. The nurse
Was known and trusted well: no reason then
To doubt her tale; nor did the doctor think
To question it, he witnessing our grief.
Yet even this deception, and the end
Attained of all my base accursed plots,
More guilty made me feel. Then Jacob swore
A solemn oath that in his arms the child
Expired or ere he left the castle walls;
But that he feared to bring it back, so rode
Along the London road a score of miles
Until he reached the Quarry Hill, and there
Down from the parapet he let it drop,
That thus the waters of the pond should hide
The little form in its secluded depths.
That was the eighth of May; I know it well.
All night I had been waiting at the tower,

And as the dawn above the hills arose
I saw him, Jacob, glide along the wall,
And knew he bore the child.   Yes, still he lives,
But in a madhouse: nay, I harmed him not;
I gave him gold and sent him to far lands,
But soon he came again, and in his arms
He ever carries ceaseless round and round
Some wisped up clothes in semblance of a child,
A babe that he declares was, years ago,
Still living, thrust into a silent pond,
Then creeping out had followed him, and begged
With piteous cry for life.   This tale he tells
To every face he sees, then wildly laughs
And says that ever since he guards it well.
And I, than he more guilty: gracious God,
Oh pardon me and him!   Since that dark day
I've never—never known a moment's peace."

   The darkness came again across his face,
The shadow of the sin; his head sank down;
O'ershrouding all his senses, fell the veil
Of deep exhaustion; while the trembling Blanche
Called Nelly to her side.   Again, once more
His dim eyes opened, and from clammy lips

Came slow the laboured words: "Send, send for her,
That I may read a pardon in her eyes;
Her mother's pardon for my hideous crime:
If it be granted to a dying wretch
In whom nought lives but penitence and grief.
Oh let her come, and I shall read my fate
Upon her lovely face. First tell her all,
Then say how I have suffered for my guilt.
Say that her right and titles she shall have;
That all the world shall know what I have done.
I would not have it otherwise. Go; go."

PART X.

THE bells that morn rang out a merry peal
 In Morland church. For, hearing that their lord
Had come at last, the ringers greeted him
With joy, according to a usance old.
But soon strange rumours came; the bells were stopped;
The ringers hastened out of church, and straight
The village folk assembled 'neath the tower,
Perplexed, and fearing unexpected ills.
In wonderment and awe the gathered throng
Asked questions of each other, till appeared
An elder dame, who in mysterious tones
Said that Lord Hollingbourne all through the night
Had lain a dying; that old Nelly Rolfe
Had nursed him, and in haste had sent for May;
That Blanche had sent express for Claud Adare,
His father's favourite son. The villagers
All clustered round the dame, (her daughter lived
As housemaid at the hall) and presently

She said, "Strange things have happened; strange
    enough,
I scarcely like to tell." But pressed upon,
And bursting with the news, she could refrain
From speech no more; the wondrous tale would out.
At first she whispered low with cautious lips,
"Our Lady May, the child we kissed and nursed
When quite a babe, like any of our own,
And felt so proud of her; we did, we did,
As she grew up—" Here weeping tears of joy,
The dame, who hitherto had spoken low,
Now with hysteric shout cried out more loud,
"Oh aye! we felt so proud of her, we did;
The fairest dearest blossom of our vale,—
To think that she, our own, own Lady May,
In her own right is Baroness Adare!"
The words pour forth so loud that all can hear;
From ear to ear, from mouth to mouth the sounds,
The startling sounds are borne with thrilling shout;
They echo from the Norman belfry tower,
And through the village street are carried on,
Till every cottage rings, while fitfully
Their wandering echoes distant hamlets catch.

And little children run with gleesome steps
Up Morland Vale to blaze the tale afar,
And seek the very spot, the High Oak Pond,
Where Lady May was found. With joyous shouts
They reach the abbey towers, and pass beneath
The cloistered shade. But there the velvet moss
So thickly grows, that as they enter in
The patter of their many feet is hushed.
This sudden silence filling them with awe,
They gaze around and clasp each other's hands,
Then hurry onwards, never looking back
Until they reach the stream near Dowling's mill.
And there they shout the tidings as they pass
The wondering miller's men, and rush on, on,
To see the very spot where Lady May
Was found by Nell so many years ago.

PART XI.

"IT must not, cannot be," said May to Blanche,
"I never will consent to his disgrace.
He wears my mother's portrait next his heart;
And great his love has been. He thought me dead,
Nor knew that Nelly, guided by a dream,
Had found and nursed me eighteen years ago.
And truly, had he known that I survived,
While yet a babe he would have found me out
And all these lands restored. And now shall I
Found strangely by his means, deprive his age
Of wealth and rule thus grown habitual,
And let him be held up to obloquy,
The father of my friends? Ah no; such rights,
As people call them, will I never take!
No, never! Let me still be little May,
Old Nelly's foundling child."

       In vain did Blanche
Her dying father's eager wishes urge,
And fears express, that if May still refused,

He could not die in peace.　May wept, and said
That he would live, and she could never bring
Contempt on him or poorer state on Blanche,
Who born in high position graced it well,
And making many happy, cared for all.

　In this dilemma Blanche consulted Claude:
But Claude was in a worse embarrassment.
His heart had long been May's; but when 'twas known
That she was Baroness Adare by right,
He passed from shapeless hope to blank dismay,
And thence into despair; for how could he
Who spoke not of his love while May was yet
The nameless foundling child of Nelly Rolfe
Declare it now, albeit then her troth
Was bound, and now 'twas free?　The open facts
Would libel him, and foulest falsehood spin
From truth and righteous honour, so that e'en
The best should scarcely choose but echo it,
So strong the lying evidence would be.

　Blanche found him buried in such thoughts as these.
At first he scarcely seemed her voice to hear,
But when she spoke the name of Lady May
He started up in attitude perplexed

That her suspicions roused. She paused awhile,
Then smiling said: "I leave it in your hands:
Neglect it not, but act. If May consent
Through your persuasion to accept her rights,
My father's suffering mind will be at rest;
Nay, this might save his life."

She left the room
Before he could refuse, nor gave him time
To make excuse. Meanwhile she knew that May
Was on the terrace, at the farther end
Reading beneath cool shadows of the trees,
And from the window where she spoke with Claude
The maiden's form distinctly could be seen.

Then Blanche went up into her father's room
To watch beside his bed. His window looked
Upon the terrace likewise, and she saw
Claude presently approach the studious May.
"That foolish boy, how slow he walks," thought she;
"He seems afraid to venture near, and yet—
I think she cares for him; if so, her wealth
Without him would to her be little worth."
She watched until he reached the seat, but then,
Too anxious e'en to look, withdrew her eyes,

As if she dimly feared that by her gaze
A spell might be dissolved. And then she knelt
Beside her father's bed.

   *   *   *   *   *   *

                      Another year,
Bearing abortive hopes and baseless fears
Into the silent land, has fleeted by;
To some unfolding brighter earthly life,
To others heavenly. Lord Hollingbourne
Still lives at Morland Hall, nor wishes more
To quit its shades beloved, (where happiness
Has dawned at last upon repentant years,)
Till carried to his grave. And even then
He hopes within its precincts fair to rest
At Morland Abbey, in the marble vault,
The ancient resting-place of the Adares.
That stately pile is now well nigh restored
With loving care by May; its pillared aisles
Are being raised again with reverence,
From slumbers sad of ruin and neglect,
To gladden village hearts. One day there came
To Claude a packet costly from far lands,
A massive chain of gold by Reuben sent,

As wedding gift for May. The owner now
Of fertile farms in yonder Southern Isle,
He wrote that he had come upon a vein,
A virgin vein of gold, on the estate,
And as the loyal token of his heart
The first-fruits did he dedicate to May.
And having heard her oft express her grief
That Morland Abbey Church should thus be left
To moulder and decay in winter winds,
He asked that she would let him send her o'er
A contribution to its rising walls,
Thank offering for his prosperity.
And soon to Nelly Rolfe a letter came
Which told the welcome news that he had found
Another virgin vein of gold—a bride,
Who made new home for him bereft of home.

  The cottage by the church has now been given
To Susan Dean; for May will never part
From Nell her second mother, who remains
At Morland Hall, and by her own desire
Inhabits there the same old nursery
Where Geraldine she reared.

     *   *   *   *   *   *

A bright May morn
Again bursts forth in beauty o'er the vale;
Again a joyous peal sounds cheerily
From out the belfry towers. Its shadow lies
In tender purples o'er the village street,
Where meet the folks in holiday attire,
And with expectant faces, greetings give.
Triumphal arches decorated gleam
At intervals along the winding road,
While Mayday garlands float upon the breeze,
And banners with the shield of the Adares.

A gay procession winds adown the vale;
Bright colours glimmer through the trees, and crowds
Of villagers, with thrilling shouts exclaim,
" Long life to Claude Adare and Lady May."

And Nelly Rolfe, the upright hearty dame
Of fourscore years and ten, is also there,
Thankful to see her darling's grandchild wed
The best and noblest of the ancient race.

www.ingramcontent.com/pod-product-compliance
Lightning Source LLC
Chambersburg PA
CBHW021943160426
43195CB00011B/1205